D1270919

Ninjas

A Guide to the Ancient Assassins

by Jessica Gunderson

Content Consultant: Michael Wert, PhD
Department of History, Marquette University
Milwaukee, Wisconsin

CAPSTONE PRESS
a capstone imprint

Velocity is published by Capstone Press,
151 Good Counsel Drive, P.O. Box 669, Mankato, Minnesota 56002.
www.capstonepub.com

Books published by Capstone Press are manufactured with paper
containing at least 10 percent post-consumer waste.

Library of Congress Cataloging-in-Publication Data
Gunderson, Jessica.
  Ninjas: a guide to the ancient assassins/by Jessica Gunderson.
    p. cm.—(Velocity: history's greatest warriors)
  Includes bibliographical references and index.
  Summary: "Profiles Ninja warriors, including their everyday life, training, fighting
methods, and societal role, as well as their place in popular culture"—Provided by
publisher.
  ISBN 978-1-4296-6600-8 (library binding)
  1. Ninja—Juvenile literature. 2. Ninjutsu—Juvenile literature. I. Title. II. Series.

UB271.J3G86 2012
355.5'48dc22   2010051695

Editorial Credits: Russell Primm
Art Director: Suzan Kadribasic
Designers: Divij Singh, Jasmeen Kaur, Manish Kumar

Photo Credits
Alamy: Gianni Dagli Orti/The Art Archive, 7 (bottom), Iain Masterton, 12, Tibor
Bognar, 13 (top left), Christian Kober/John Warburton-Lee Photography, 13 (right), Chris
Willson, 18-19, 37, MicaTravel2, 22, Shoosmith Jersey Beach Collection, 24-25, Photo
Japan, 32-33, Tony French, 42; Corbis: Bloomimage, 1, Asian Art & Archaeology, Inc.,
38, 39; Getty Images: BLOOM image, cover, Knauer/Johnston, 14, Chase Jarvis, 23,
26, 29, Kazuhiro Nogi/AFP, 44-45; Granger Collection, NYC: 9; Istockphoto: Milorad
Zaric, 5, Steven Wynn, 7 (back), Niko Guido, 15, Ethan Myerson, 16; PhotoGuide Japan:
Philbert Ono, 28; Rex Features: Everett, 41, SNAP, 43; Shutterstock: Nelic, design element
(shuriken), Jef Thompson, 10, High Leg Studio, 11, Jecka, 21, Dmitrijs Bindemanis, 27,
Neale Cousland, 30-31, Konstantin Sutyagin, 30-31 (fire), Vule, 34-35.

Printed in the United States of America in Melrose Park, Illinois.
032011   006112LKF11

TABLE of CONTENTS

CHAPTER 1

SECRET WARRIORS

Death by Ninja

Ninja legends are whispered in darkness and passed down through the ages. Murder and **espionage** fill these tales. One legend tells of the murder of Uesugi Kenshin in 1577.

Kenshin was a powerful man with many enemies. He kept guards around him at all times. But even in dangerous times, a man needs time alone—especially when visiting the bathroom.

As the story goes, one night Kenshin approached his outhouse. He went inside and shut the door. He didn't know that a ninja **assassin** was crouched in the sewer beneath the toilet. As Kenshin sat down, the ninja speared his bottom with a sword. Kenshin fell to the floor, twisting in pain. The ninja slipped away into the night.

Kenshin died several days later. The details of what happened that night died with him. But everyone whispered about his many enemies. And within their whispers was a terrifying word: ninja.

Kenshin's assassination by a ninja is likely just a rumor. Still, it has become a legend that fits the popular idea of a ninja warrior. What comes to mind when you hear the word ninja? Most people think of a shadowy figure shrouded in black; one who will stop at nothing to carry out his task. Stories like Kenshin's have kept the ninja myth alive. They make ninja seem almost **superhuman.**

espionage—the practice of spying
assassin—someone who kills a person of importance, either for pay or for a cause
superhuman—having powers, qualities, or skills beyond typical human beings

THE ORIGIN OF THE NINJA

Power Struggle

Throughout the 1400s, Japan was a restless land. Wars between rulers raged. Everyone wanted power. But who was really the most powerful?

The **emperor** boasted that he was the ruler of Japan. And he was, officially. He owned a palace and an army. In reality, the emperor had little say in the governing of Japan. That responsibility was the shogun's.

The **shogun** was the general of the emperor's army. The country would fall into confusion if the shogun's power weakened. The shogun was always looking over his shoulder for the daimyo. The daimyo desired the shogun's power.

Daimyo were local rulers throughout Japan. They ruled their lands any way they liked. They cared little for the emperor's wishes. They sometimes ignored the shogun's orders. Daimyo were greedy for more land and wealth. They often fought against one another. Many daimyo hoped to overthrow the shogun and take over Japan. But they didn't like to get their hands dirty with fighting. Instead, they hired samurai and ninja for that task. They filled the ranks with peasants and other commoners to increase the size of their armies.

Samurai warriors were the visible warriors for the daimyo. They were wealthy and belonged to a high social class. They were bound by contract to a daimyo. As warriors, they had the honor of status and recognition.

Ninja also worked for the daimyo, but they did so in secrecy. They carried out secret missions such as assassinations. To them, money was more important than loyalty. But success was important too, and they would do anything necessary to succeed in their missions.

ancient Japanese emperor

a Japanese daimyo

7

The Art of
Ninjutsu

Most historians relate the ninja to the set of fighting skills called ninjutsu. Ninjutsu developed in the Iga and Koga regions of Japan.

Defeated Japanese warriors from battles in the town of Kyoto hid in Iga and Koga. They continued to practice their fighting skills.

Some historians believe that immigrants from other countries influenced ninjutsu. Some people from Korea moved to Iga and Koga. They brought new ideas about religion and fighting with them.

Chinese merchants and immigrants also lived in the region. They practiced Chinese fighting methods.

It is possible that Japanese ninja warriors were influenced by the beliefs and practices of Korean and Chinese immigrants. Over time their fighting skills became known as ninjutsu.

FACT:

The most important ninjutsu skill was the knowledge of self. A ninja had to be in tune with his strengths and weaknesses.

Tengu

According to legend, ninja first learned their skills from demons called *tengu*. A tengu was a half-bird, half-man who lived in trees. A tengu often clothed himself in disguises and tried to confuse his enemies.

Ninja vs. Samurai

Ninja and samurai were both warriors in medieval Japan. But the two couldn't be more different. How well do you know the ninja? How about the samurai?

Ninja:

- Deceitful
- Wore disguises
- Would work for anyone who paid him
- Willing to spy
- Came from common families
- Worked for more than one daimyo
- Broke into castles

FACT:

A daimyo would use a ninja to do things that his samurai were forbidden to do. The samurai code of honor prevented spying and sneak attacks.

Samurai:

- Was supposed to follow a **strict code of honor**
- Came from a wealthy family
- Sometimes loyal to his daimyo
- Refused to do anything dishonorable
- Would not dress as a common villager

FACT:

A samurai sometimes hired a ninja to do his dirty work. A samurai's enemy might also hire the same ninja. A smart samurai regarded his ninja with suspicion and fear.

A SECRET LIFE

The Many Faces of Ninja

You probably picture a man shrouded in black when you think of a ninja. Only his eyes show. He creeps slowly along. He blends in with dark buildings and crouches among shrubs. When he meets his enemy, his eyes glow. The enemy is frozen in fear by the sight of two eyes hanging in the dark.

This idea of the ninja is only partly correct. Ninja may have worn black garb, but only for certain nighttime tasks. They usually wore camouflage to blend in with trees or the bricks of a building.

During the day, ninja wanted to blend in with the crowd. They didn't want to draw attention to themselves. Their disguises were simply the clothing of others around them. Deception was the foundation of ninja life.

A ninja dressed as a traveling merchant had an excuse for his accent. He could carry weapons in his merchant cart.

A ninja dressed as a traveling monk or priest could gain trust. People trusted religious men and allowed them into their homes. Dressed as a wandering samurai, a ninja could carry weapons openly.

camouflage—fabric that matches the surroundings

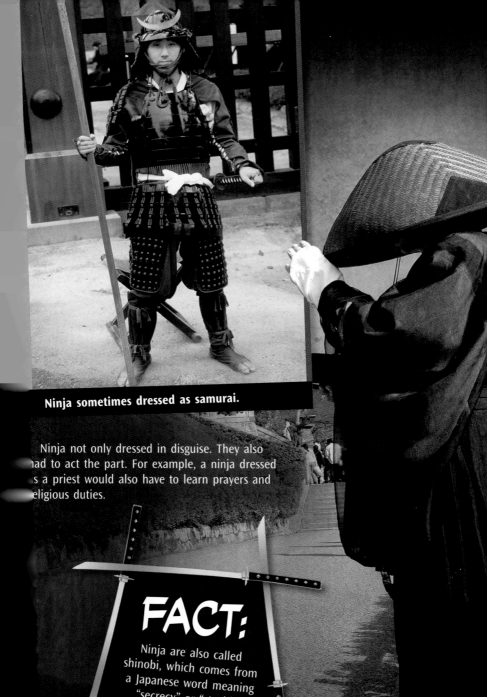

Ninja sometimes dressed as samurai.

Ninja not only dressed in disguise. They also had to act the part. For example, a ninja dressed as a priest would also have to learn prayers and religious duties.

FACT:

Ninja are also called shinobi, which comes from a Japanese word meaning "secrecy" or "stealth."

Kid Warriors

Ninja fathers taught their children the tricks of the trade. Training began when the child was 5 years old or even younger. Exercises helped ninja children learn balance and agility. They also worked on developing **stamina**.

Good balance helped ninja walk along narrow places or along walls of buildings without fear of falling. Ninja children learned balance by walking on a long, skinny log raised off the ground. They practiced running, jumping, turning, and sitting on the log without falling off. The log was raised higher as a child became more skilled.

Ninja children also learned to run fast for long distances. A special kind of straw hat measured speed. Children placed the hat on their chests and ran as fast as they could. The force of the wind would keep the hat on his or her chest if the child ran fast enough. If the hat fell off, the child was too slow. Ninja children learned how to use weapons, poisons, and explosives when they were teenagers.

Children learn ninjutsu fighting techniques.

stamina—the energy and strength to keep doing something for a long

Kunoichi

Female ninja were called kunoichi. No one usually suspected a woman of being a ninja. Kunoichi could hide weapons in their elaborate hairstyles or dresses. They also used their fans as weapons.

FACT:

Ninja often walked sideways. Why? So no one would know which way a ninja was going if his tracks were discovered.

Spy Secrets

Each ninja family or group developed its own traditions. These traditions were called ryū. The ryū were passed down along ninja family lines or from a ninja to his student. The knowledge and methods of a particular ryū were written down.

Ninja did not want their secrets revealed or stolen by other ninja. They wrote them in secret code or confusing wording. Often only the ninjas within the ryū could understand the scrolls.

Secret Recipes

Sometimes ninja had to travel long distances without much food or water. They used secret recipes to make pills that quenched thirst or curbed hunger. Did the pills actually work? That's another ninja secret.

Below is a recipe for pills developed to reduce a ninja's hunger.

- 40 parts ginseng
- 80 parts flour
- 80 parts buckwheat flower
- 80 parts mountain potato
- 4 parts chickweed
- 40 yokui kernels
- 80 parts glutinous rice

Soak mixture in rice wine for three years. Roll mixture into a ball. Take three a day.

Home Is Where the Danger Is

A ninja tried to keep his identity secret, sometimes even from some members of his own family. But he was always aware that his identity could be discovered. A ninja was always in danger of being attacked in his own home.

Many ninja turned their homes into hideouts with secret passageways and closets. They knew that their lives could be in danger and they might need to act quickly.

Ninja homes looked like normal houses from the outside and on the inside. But a ninja home had just as many secrets as its owner:

- Loose floorboards kept weapons hidden and within reach.

- Fake hallways leading to dead ends could confuse an assailant.

- Guards could hide in secret wall panels and emerge if the ninja was in danger.

- Secret doors in the wall or trap doors on the floor led to underground tunnels.

- Staircases disguised as shelves allowed quick escape.

Ninja-Proofing

Many daimyo installed squeaky "nightingale floors" to catch ninja intruders. Some placed paper over the floor that would crackle if stepped on. Another technique was to cover sections between stairs with thin paper. A guard could hide behind the wall or under the stairs and quickly thrust a sword at an intruder.

仏聖殿

CHAPTER 4

WEAPONS

A Weapon in the Hand

A ninja had to master many types of weapons. Often he used any nearby object, such as a table or a rope, to defend himself. If a ninja carried weapons with him, they were usually small and easily hidden. Ninja used short swords. They were easier to carry and allowed for better mobility.

A sword's scabbard served multiple purposes. Sometimes the ninja carried small tools in the scabbard. Some scabbards could be used as underwater breathing tubes.

A kusarigama was a blade with a short handle and weighted chain. The ninja used the kusarigama's blade to slash or stab his enemy. He used the chain to swing at the enemy or to lasso the enemy's body or weapon.

shuriken

A shuriken, or throwing knife, was a valuable ninja weapon. The ninja could launch the shuriken at his pursuer. The shuriken usually didn't kill the enemy, but it could injure him enough to give the ninja time to get away.

Tekagi were a bit like medieval brass knuckles. The ninja could conceal tekagi easily and catch his opponent by surprise. The enemy would barely have time to notice what hit him before the ninja escaped.

scabbard—a protective case for a sword, knife, or dagger

scabbard

short sword

FACT:

Props used for the ninja's disguise could double as weaponry. A walking stick or shovel could easily be used against an enemy.

The Escape Artist

No one would hire a well-known ninja. A ninja had to be anonymous and able to blend in with the crowd. To help hide their identities, ninja avoided attacks from their enemies. They used various tools to help them escape quickly.

Caltrops were spiked devices that could be thrown in the pursuer's path. The caltrop always landed with one spike up. The nail would stab the pursuer's foot and slow him down.

Smoke bombs produced a spark and smoke. The ninja would be gone by the time the smoke cleared.

Ninja sometimes used **sprays** similar to today's pepper spray, directing them at an enemy's eyes. The spray blinded the enemy temporarily and gave the ninja enough time to run away.

FACT:

Ninja also "became inhuman" to escape from enemies by pretending to be a rock, bush, or tree.

A **shuko** was an iron-spiked band worn around the hand. It was also called "tiger's claws." A shuko could be used to swipe the opponent's face in hand-to-hand fighting. A shuko may also have helped ninja climb walls or trees.

Body Dynamics

Fu no kata means "fighting like the wind." This ninjutsu technique of self-defense is still practiced today. It is based on traditional methods used by ninjas and uses speed and agility to escape from violent attacks. In fu no kata, the ninja flows around his attacker. By not being where the attacker anticipates he will be, the ninja avoids injury. Here is one possible fighting technique:

A. The ninja jumps to his left to avoid the attacker's punch.

B. Then the ninja jabs his arm into the joint of the attacker's punching arm.

C. The attacker's arm swings upward.

D. When the attacker sends a second punch, the ninja jumps to the left.

E. Now the ninja is out of the attacker's sight.

F. The ninja can now slam the attacker's jaw and bring him down with a knee jab from behind.

A modern-day teacher demonstrates a ninjutsu self-defense technique.

Ninja made signs with their fingers, called mudra, in order to **hypnotize** their enemies or to pretend to summon ghosts of warriors. These signs added to the ninja mystique and were effective in frightening the enemy.

hypnotize—to put someone into a state in which the person appears to be asleep but can still respond to suggestions and answer questions

Shrouded in Myth

The greatest of all ninja weapons was fear. Throughout Japan people heard rumors of the ninja and their **supernatural** abilities. People feared the ninja.

Ninja didn't try to stop the rumors. They knew they could use fear to their advantage.

supernatural—something that cannot be explained by science or logic

Rumor	**Truth**
✳ Ninja could disappear in a puff of smoke.	Ninja used smoke bombs to create a bright light and smoke and could then run away or hide.
✳ Ninja were not human; they were ghosts.	Ninja sometimes faked their own deaths and then "rose from the dead."
✳ Ninja could fly.	A group of ninja sometimes formed a pyramid to hoist one ninja over a castle wall. The people inside the castle couldn't see the pyramid, just the one ninja.
✳ Ninja could multiply.	Often several ninja would invade a castle at once, each wearing the same clothing.
✳ Ninja could breathe underwater.	Ninja used a long, hollow reed as a breathing tube.
✳ Ninja could walk on water.	Ninja used floating devices to help them cross water without getting wet.

Ninja Clothing

A ninja was often in disguise. But when he wasn't, he wore special clothing to help him on his secret missions. The ninja's garb was usually a dark color, such as dark blue or green. It often had these features:

A belt used to help climb trees or buildings.

Pockets to hold tools or weapons.

A hood to conceal his identity.

Claws on his feet to help him climb.

A ninja might also have worn light body armor under his clothing. Small, rectangular metal plates could have been sewn onto a cloth garment. This construction would have given the ninja mobility and protection.

FACT:

Some ninja wore dark red clothing. The color hid bloodstains so the enemy wouldn't know if the ninja was hurt.

NINJA STRATEGY

Ninja loved to use fire as a weapon. Fires, even small ones, caused confusion and panic.

In 1541 ninja warriors surrounded a castle. They hid in bushes and trees and waited for their chance to break in. The ninja crept toward a nearby temple. They threw burning sticks and matches on it. Soon the temple was in flames. The confusion caused by the fire allowed the ninja warriors to quickly and easily enter the castle.

In 1558 ninja working for the daimyo Rokkaku Yoshikata approached an enemy castle. Guards surrounded the castle. There were too many for the ninja to overthrow. Each guard carried a lantern with the family symbol on it. This gave the ninja an idea. They stole one of the guard's lanterns. Then they snuck away and made lanterns just like the ones the guards carried. When they returned, they blended in with the crowd. They marched into the castle, where they immediately launched a fiery attack.

Capture the Castle

Breaking into an enemy castle was a common ninja mission. But castles were often heavily **fortified**. Guards stood at the top of the castle walls, watching for intruders. At night lanterns glowed along the rims of castle walls. How could ninja break into such a protected place?

One strategy was to shoot a primitive rifle, called an arquebus, at a lantern. The guards would rush to extinguish all the lanterns, fearing the castle was under attack by an enemy army. They wanted to make the castle as dark as possible so the enemy couldn't see what they were aiming at. In the darkness the ninja would slip inside the castle unnoticed. Meanwhile, the guards waited outside for another rifle shot. When they heard no more shots, the guards lit the lanterns again. By then, the ninja were already inside the castle, carrying out their spying mission or assassination.

FACT:

Ninja also used their athletic skills to enter castles. They might swing over a castle's moat on a rope or shimmy along thin castle walls.

fortified—strengthened by defenses such as walls and guards

Spy Network

Not all ninja were alike. Ninja had different roles in the spy network.

The **Man from the Moon** lived in enemy territory. He made friends with the locals and recruited them to do some dirty work for him.

The **Firefly Glimmer** would allow himself to be caught by the enemy. Then he would make false accusations about those on the enemy's side, creating suspicion among the enemy's forces.

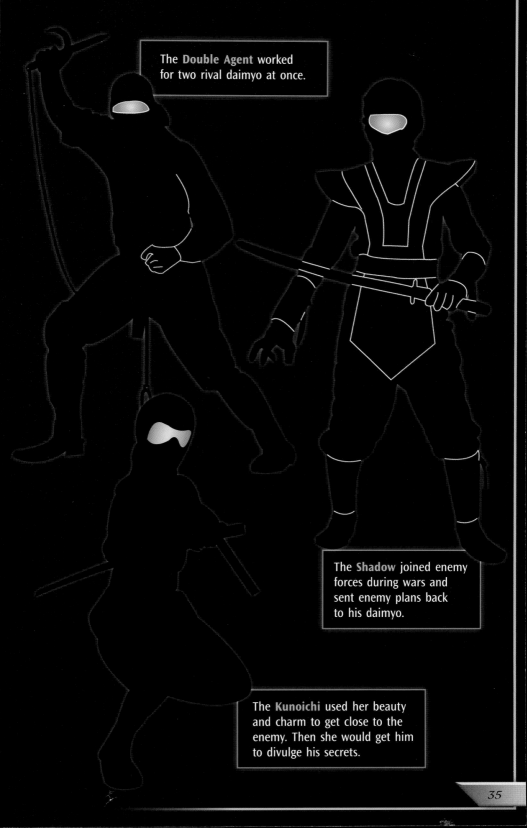

The **Double Agent** worked for two rival daimyo at once.

The **Shadow** joined enemy forces during wars and sent enemy plans back to his daimyo.

The **Kunoichi** used her beauty and charm to get close to the enemy. Then she would get him to divulge his secrets.

The Ninja Disappear

Oda Nobunaga and Tokugawa Ieyasu were rival daimyo. Both men wanted to control all of Japan. Oda felt that ninja stood in the way of his goals, especially in the Iga province. The ninja there had thrown out the daimyo. They ruled the province themselves. Oda wanted to destroy Iga.

Oda sent his best warriors to attack Iga in 1579. The ninja fought them off. Two years later Oda's men attacked again. This time they defeated the ninja. Many ninja fled the province after their defeat. Tokugawa helped some of them hide from Oda. In return they agreed to work for him.

In 1582 another rival daimyo, Akechi Mitsuhide, had his warriors kill Oda. Tokugawa knew he was next on Akechi's hit list. At that time, Tokugawa was in the Osaka province. He had to travel through Iga to return to his home in Mikawa. He knew Akechi's men would try to ambush him along the way.

One of Tokugawa's ninja warriors, Hattori Hanzo, offered to help. He traveled ahead of Tokugawa through Iga, recruiting the ninja who were still there. By the time Tokugawa reached Iga, Hattori had gathered 200 ninja. The ninja protected Tokugawa from Akechi's warriors.

Tokugawa went on to become shogun of Japan. He was such a strong leader that the wars between daimyo ceased. Daimyo no longer needed to hire ninja. The ninja culture soon faded away.

a statue of Tokugawa Ieyasu

CHAPTER 6

NINJA CRAZE

Japanese Folklore

The ninja, with their mysterious and secret ways, became legends in Japan. Ninja warriors have been illustrated, painted, and sculpted. Popular folklore tells of superhuman ninja and their mystical feats.

In one popular story, Jiraiya was a ninja who stole from the rich and gave to the poor. He used his magical powers to change into a giant toad. His greatest enemy was Orochimaru, a snake magician. Orochimaru was also a ninja. Their conflict lasted several years before Jiraiya finally defeated Orochimaru.

Legendary outlaw Ishikawa Goemon was said to have been skilled in ninjutsu. Many **kabuki** plays are based on his life. He is also the subject of a 2009 Japanese movie. As a young man, he sets off to avenge his master's death, robbing the rich along the way.

In a scene from a kabuki play, an actor portrays Ishikawa Goemon as he holds his son.

kabuki—traditional Japanese dramatic performances with singing and dancing

Ninja Cinema

Koga Unôn Ninjutsu Kogaryû was a Japanese silent film released in 1916. It was possibly the first movie about ninja warriors. *Torawakamaru the Koga Ninja* is another Japanese film featuring ninja. It was released in 1957.

One of the first American films to feature ninja was *You Only Live Twice*, a 1967 James Bond film. In the film, a spacecraft mysteriously disappears. British intelligence agents believe it is in the Sea of Japan. James Bond is sent to Japan to investigate. He trains with a group of ninja, learning ninjutsu and Japanese language and culture. Bond then disguises himself as a Japanese fisherman in order to discover the whereabouts of the spacecraft.

Ninja Assassin, a 2009 film, tells the story of Raizo, an orphan who is taken in by the Ozuno Clan ninja. He is trained to become a ninja assassin. After a betrayal turns his clan against him, he goes on the run.

Naruto is a Japanese comic book series about a young ninja who aspires to be a Hokage, a village ninja leader. In 2002 *Naruto* was made into a popular Japanese **anime** television series. In the United States, the series aired on the Cartoon Network. *Naruto* was so popular that it spawned seven feature-length films and many video games. In the video games, a player controls one of the characters from the series and engages in fighting against other characters. Two popular games released in North America are *Naruto: Clash of Ninja* and *Naruto: Ninja Council.*

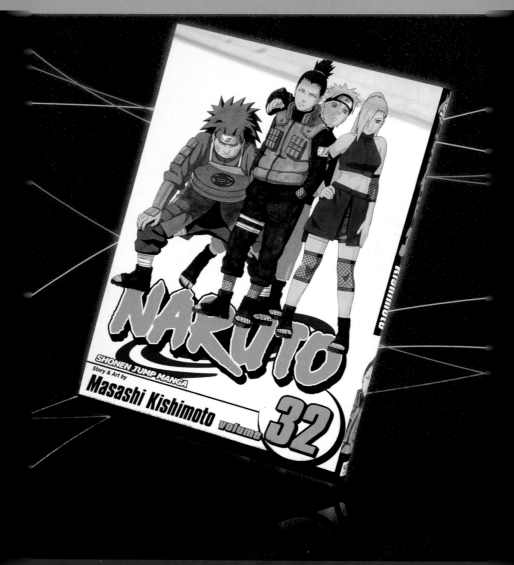

anime—a Japanese style of animation, often with colorful art

Turtle Power! **Teenage Mutant Ninja Turtles** is a popular cartoon series featuring four turtles that were trained in ninjutsu by their mutant rat master. They live in the sewers of New York City and fight criminals.

Raphael wears a red mask. He is an aggressive turtle that loves to fight. His weapon is a pair of sai, sharp Japanese daggers.

Michelangelo is the fun-loving, humorous turtle. He wears an orange mask and wields a nunchaku, a weapon of two sticks connected by a short chain.

Leonardo is the leader of the turtle pack. He wears a blue mask and carries two katana swords.

Donatello is the thinker. He prefers to solve crimes using his intelligence instead of violence. He carries a bo staff, a long wooden weapon, and wears a purple mask.

katana sword—a long, curved Japanese sword

Ninja Culture

Do ninja warriors exist today? Maybe not as secret assassins, but the art of ninjutsu lives on. Masaaki Hatsumi is the 34th Grandmaster of Ninjutsu. How do you become a grandmaster? It isn't easy.

A master ninja teaches his students techniques and tactics and names one student as grandmaster. When that grandmaster grows old, he names one of his students to be the new grandmaster. Masaaki Hatsumi is the 34th in the line of ninja grandmasters. He teaches students to use ninjutsu techniques for self-defense.

FACT:
Stephen K. Hayes was Masaaki Hatsumi's first American student. Hayes now teaches ninjutsu in the United States.

FACT:
Iga's mayor and city council members dress up like ninja for a session they call Ninja Congress.

Some tourists dress in ninja costumes at the annual ninja festival in Iga.

Every spring, more than 30,000 tourists flock to Iga for the annual ninja festival. The festival features parades, competitions, and performances. During the festival, you can dress up in ninja garb and try your hand at throwing shuriken. You can also join the hunt for hidden ninja mannequins.

GLOSSARY

anime (AN-i-may)—a Japanese style of animation, often with colorful art

assassin (uh-SASS-in)—someone who kills a person of importance, either for pay or for a cause

camouflage (KAM-uh-flahzh)—fabric that matches the surroundings

espionage (ESS-pee-uh-nahzh)—the practice of spying

fortified (FOR-tuh-fyed)—strengthened by defenses such as walls and guards

hypnotize (HIP-nuh-tize)—to put someone into a state in which the person appears to be asleep but is still able to respond to suggestions and answer questions

kabuki (kuh-BOO-kee)—traditional Japanese dramatic performances with singing and dancing

katana sword (kah-TAH-nah SORD)—a long, curved Japanese sword

scabbard (SKAB-urd)—a protective case for a sword, knife, or dagger

stamina (STAM-uh-nuh)—the energy and strength to keep doing something for a long time

superhuman (soo-pur-HYOO-muhn)—having powers, qualities, or skills beyond typical human beings

supernatural (soo-pur-NACH-ur-uhl)—something that cannot be explained by science or logic

READ MORE

Doeden, Matt. *Life as a Ninja: An Interactive History Adventure*. Warriors. Mankato, Minn.: Capstone Press, 2010.

Glaser, Jason. *Ninja*. Warriors of History. Mankato, Minn.: Capstone Press, 2006.

Turnbull, Stephen. *Real Ninja: Over 20 True Stories of Japan's Secret Assassins*. New York: Enchanted Lion Books, 2008.

INTERNET SITES

FactHound offers a safe, fun way to find Internet sites related to this book. All of the sites on FactHound have been researched by our staff.

Here's all you do:

Visit *www.facthound.com*

Type in this code: 9781429666008

INDEX